A New True Book

THE ONEIDA

By Jill Duvall

CHILDRENS PRESS ®
CHICAGO

© 1990 Steve Wall

PHOTO CREDITS

The Bettmann Archive—27 (left), 38 (left)

© Reinhard Brucker—12 (2 photos), 14, 17 (right), 18, 24

H. Armstrong Roberts—27 (right); © Charles Phelps Cushing, 31

© Gloria Halbritter—5, 17 (left), 19, 37 (left), 42 (2 photos), 45 (2 photos); © Joe Winn, 43

Historical Pictures Service—7, 29

National Museum of American Art, Washington, DC/Art Resource, NY—21

North Wind Picture Archives—9

Photograph Courtesy of Smithsonian Institution National Museum of the American Indian—33, 34, 38 (left)

© 1990 Steve Wall—Cover, 2, 23, 37 (right), 40, 41

© John Kahionhes Fadden—10

Cover—Oneida woman and child in traditional dress (© 1990 Steve Wall)

Iroquois child holding
a corn-husk doll

Library of Congress Cataloging-in-Publication Data

Duvall, Jill D.
    The Oneida / by Jill D. Duvall.
        p.   cm. — (A New true book)
    Includes index.
    Summary: Describes the history, culture, and
changing fortunes of the Oneida Indians.
    ISBN 0-516-01125-1
    1.   Oneida Indians—Juvenile literature.
[1.   Oneida Indians.   2.   Indians of North America.]
I.   Title.
E99.045D88   1991   91-8893
973'.04975—dc20   CIP
                                            AC

TABLE OF CONTENTS

Old and New Worlds...4

The Iroquois Confederacy...8

Oneida Written History...11

Village Life...13

Newcomers...19

Reverend Samuel Kirkland...25

Troubled Times...28

Moving West...31

Change in Wisconsin...35

New York Oneida...40

More Good News...43

Words You Should Know...46

Index...47

OLD AND NEW WORLDS

The Europeans who first explored North America said they had found a "new world." But it wasn't new. Many people, including the Oneida, were already there. The trails that led to the Oneida villages and towns were well traveled, sometimes by visitors from far-away places.

The Oneida called

4

The Oneida Standing Stone

themselves Onayotekaono
(oh•nah•yoh•tee•kah•oh•no),
which means "People of
the Standing Stone." An
Oneida legend says a
certain stone always
showed them the way to

go. Good land, clear water, and plenty of food were found wherever the stone directed, the legend said.

Oneidas lived in villages with many longhouses. When there was danger, wooden walls were built around a town. When the danger passed, visitors were welcomed.

Farm fields lay outside each village. When the land

This drawing of an old Oneida village shows women
preparing food while men build a longhouse.

had been farmed long enough,
the villagers moved on. In
this way, the soil and the
forests did not suffer from
too much human use.

THE IROQUOIS CONFEDERACY

In the 1500s, European settlers learned about a group of Native Americans that they called the Iroquois Confederacy. The Iroquois called themselves the Haudenosaunee (hoe•dee•noh•SAW•nee) "People of the Longhouse." The Iroquois Confederacy was made up of five nations, the Seneca, Oneida, Cayuga, Onondaga, and

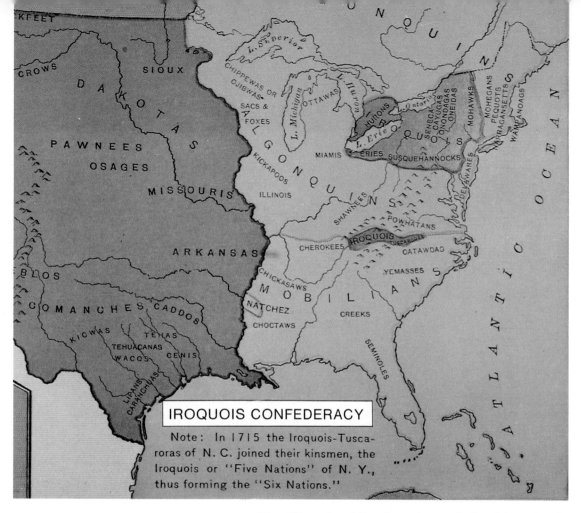

The "People of the Longhouse" lived in what is now the northeastern United States.

Mohawk. They lived next to each other in what is now New York State. The Oneida land was between Mohawk and Onondaga territories.

9

Seneca   Tuscarora   Cayuga   Onondaga   Oneida   Mohawk

© John Kahionhes Fadden

In this drawing by John Kahionhes Fadden, the longhouse represents the Haudenosaunee, or Iroquois Confederacy. The arrangement of the eagle feathers on each hat, called a Gustoweh, identifies each member nation. From left to right: the Seneca, one vertical feather; the Tuscarora, no feather; the Cayuga, one feather, angled back; the Onondaga, two feathers; the Oneida, two upright feathers, and one angled down; and the Mohawk, three upright feathers. The Tuscarora became the sixth member of the Iroquois Confederacy in early 1700s.

The Iroquois Confederacy was a peace league. The members agreed not to fight each other. Representatives from the member nations held meetings and made decisions for the Confederacy.

ONEIDA
WRITTEN HISTORY

The Oneida, like all Native Americans, memorized their history. In winter, trained storytellers traveled from village to village. They talked about recent news and ancient history.

Children learned their clan's history from the storytellers and their mothers. Skill in reciting the stories was greatly honored by the Iroquois.

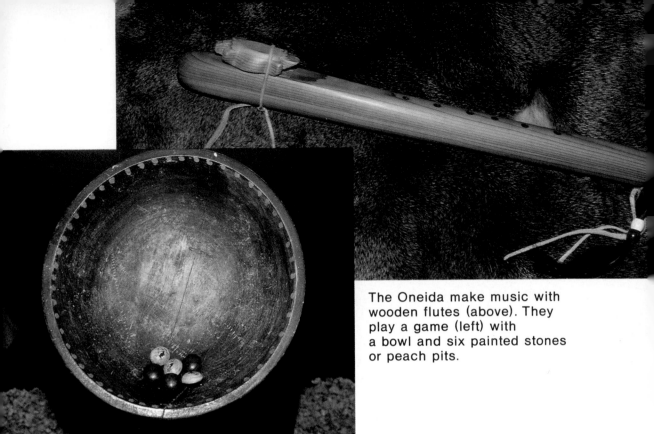

The Oneida make music with wooden flutes (above). They play a game (left) with a bowl and six painted stones or peach pits.

The earliest written record of the Oneida was left by a Dutch writer named Harmen Meyndertsz van den Bogaert. He arrived in the Oneida village on December 30, 1634.

VILLAGE LIFE

The village van den Bogaert described was peaceful. Food was plentiful. Friendship was extended to the Dutchman.

Many families lived within the village walls. They lived in clusters of longhouses.

The longhouses were sometimes over 300 feet long. They were built on a framework of poles cut

There were several cooking fires surrounded by stones in each longhouse.

from trees and stuck in the ground. The poles were curved at the top to form rafters, or supports for the roof. The whole building was covered with tree bark. Several families lived in each longhouse.

Long ago, and even today,
every Oneida person belonged
to a clan. A clan is like a
large family. The Oneidas
have three clans. Each clan
is named after an animal.
There is a bear clan,
a wolf clan, and a turtle clan.

The women who lived in a
longhouse were sisters,
mothers, or daughters of the

same clan. The fathers were from a different clan. A totem, or picture, of the clan's animal hung over the longhouse door.

Senior women were the leaders of their clans. They chose the men who would be chiefs and who would represent the nation at meetings of the Confederacy.

Mary Cornelius Winder (left) of the Wolf Clan
was a famous Oneida basketmaker.
Oneida baskets (above) were used to store
food and household items.

The Oneida were famous
for their skill in fishing. Fish
were traded with nations
throughout the area. The
women also did the planting
and harvesting of crops.
They grew corn, squash, and

The Oneida made colorful woven belts.

beans. The men hunted and protected the village. The children learned skills from the older people.

Van den Bogaert admired the Oneidas' way of doing things and their friendliness. He was most impressed with the strong love they had for their land.

Oneidas reenact fur trading with the Europeans
at Fort Stanwix, New York, in 1978.

NEWCOMERS

Europeans began coming
to the Haudenosaunee
lands in the 1600s. At
first, the newcomers
wanted only furs. But they
found the land so beautiful
that they wanted to stay.

19

More and more foreigners came. Disputes began. The Haudenosaunee tried to stay out of these fights.

Misfortunes began to come to the Native Americans. Disease and war killed many. Colonists took over their lands. Trees were cut down. Game was no longer plentiful.

The Dutch, French, and English all wanted the Haudenosaunee to join in their fights with each other.

This painting of Bread, an Oneida chief, was made by the American artist George Catlin in 1831.

The law of the Iroquois Confederacy said that all the member nations must agree on declarations of war. If any nation said no, the league could not fight as a single force.

The law also said that each nation could make its own decisions. If a nation decided on war, however, it was on its own.

During the American Revolution, American colonists fought against their British rulers. Some Native Americans were forced to take sides. The British had made many friends with the Iroquois Confederacy. When the American colonies

Today, the Oneida
continue
traditional ways.

revolted, the Haudenosaunee
thought of it as a war
between brothers. But the
Haudenosaunee were not
able to stay neutral for
long. Nor could they agree
on which side to help.

Iroquois
weapons

Most of the Oneida
chose to help the "new
Americans." A sad part
of the Oneida legend of
the Standing Stone was
coming true. The stone could
not show the way if the
people were divided.

REVEREND SAMUEL KIRKLAND

Many Oneida sided with the colonists because of the Reverend Samuel Kirkland. This missionary had lived among the Oneida for twelve years when the American Revolution began. Many Oneida had become Christian converts.

Peter Shenandoah was a Christian. He was a close friend of the missionary. Kirkland convinced many Oneida, including Shenandoah, to take the colonists' side.

Before long, the Oneida and the Tuscarora, who recently joined the Iroquois league, were fighting other members of the league.

Sir William Johnson, the British Crown's

Sir William Johnson

Superintendent of
Indian Affairs had been fair
with the Iroquois
and had won their respect.
Because of Sir William,
many Iroquois sided with
the British.

TROUBLED TIMES

During and after the American Revolution, the Oneida were divided on many issues. Some abandoned their traditional ways. The system of government by chiefs was challenged. Clan mothers no longer chose chiefs. Villages were burned. Many Oneida were driven from their ancestral lands.

George Washington was the first president of the United States.

When George Washington became president in 1789, he promised the Oneida and Tuscarora a homeland. The new United States laws said no Indian lands could be sold without approval of Congress.

However, the Haudenosaunee never agreed to seek the approval of the U.S. government on matters concerning their own government. Before long, many illegal deals had left the Oneida and Tuscarora nearly without land. The settlers in New York State took over much of the Oneida territory.

Eleazar
Williams

MOVING WEST

Eleazer Williams, a
Mohawk, was a Christian
missionary. In the early
1820s, Reverend Williams
led a group of Oneida to a

reservation at Duck Creek, Wisconsin. This move was part of the United States government's plan to move all Indians west.

Many promises made to the Native Americans were broken during this time. Forest fires, smallpox, poverty, and war had killed many thousands.

In 1887, the U.S. Congress passed the General Allotment Act. This law was designed to encourage Indians as individuals and to destroy all tribal governments.

Oneida longhouse built of logs

Some Oneida stayed in
New York. Most of their
land was taken away. Some
were given money to sign
papers that said they had
sold their land. Although
the Oneida nation said
these sales were illegal, the
government did nothing. As
a result, the Oneida

Oneidas in a log longhouse, photographed in 1907.

scattered further apart.

In 1924, the United States allowed all Native Americans to become citizens. The Oneida had their own government. They decided not to become U.S. citizens.

CHANGE IN WISCONSIN

It seemed the Oneida
would disappear as so
many other Eastern tribes
had done. Then, their
fortunes began to change.

Good leadership began
to rebuild Oneida government.
The people worked hard
to improve life at the
Wisconsin reservation.

Under President Franklin
D. Roosevelt, the Indian
Reorganization Act was
passed in 1934.

The Oneida used the
funds from this act well.
They built houses and set
up businesses, schools,
and churches. Committees
were set up to settle land,
water, health, and
education questions. A
constitution was written.
Men and women could vote
and hold public office.

The Wisconsin Oneidas
have been buying back
land since the 1930s.
Governing headquarters
and industrial parks have

Wilson Cornelius (left), a member of the Oneida Bear Clan, wrote letters to the United States government about Oneida land claims in the early 1900s. Oneida women (right) in traditional dress

been added to the reservation.

After the 1950s, Oneida reorganization again began to work well. Some of the leaders who worked very

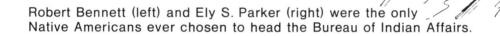

Robert Bennett (left) and Ely S. Parker (right) were the only Native Americans ever chosen to head the Bureau of Indian Affairs.

hard to make the nation stronger were Irene Moore, Oscar Archiquette, and Purcell Powless.

In 1967, Robert R. Bennett, an Oneida, was

chosen by President Lyndon B. Johnson to head the U.S. Bureau of Indian Affairs (BIA). Only one other Native American had ever served in that position before. That was Ely S. Parker, a Seneca. He, too, was an Iroquois.

Once the Oneida had been the smallest nation in the Iroquois Confederacy. Now there are more than 10,000 people living on Oneida lands in Wisconsin.

A group of Oneida women plant corn on Oneida territory in New York State.

NEW YORK ONEIDA

In 1784, Governor Clinton of New York described Oneida territory. There were at least 6 million acres. Now there are 32 acres.

Still, the few Oneida who remained in New York have descendants living on

40

Clan Mother
Maisie Shenandoah
and her daughters
inspect the
new longhouse
under construction.

that tiny bit of their ancestral land. The Standing Stone is still there.

After a very long time, some traditional Indian ways are coming back. For the first time in over 150 years, there is a longhouse on Oneida territory in New York. The house is used for councils and ceremonies.

41

The Oneida bingo hall (top) brings in millions of dollars for the Oneida reservation. The cookhouse (bottom) is used for meetings and to prepare food for ceremonies.

The greatest change is economic. In 1985, the New York Oneida built a bingo hall. Now the tiny reservation makes millions of dollars every year.

MORE GOOD NEWS

Oneida attorneys are using United States laws to reverse Oneida misfortunes. In 1974, they won a great victory.

Arthur "Ray" Halbritter, an Oneida, graduated from Harvard Law School. He believes that Native Americans can live in the modern world and still keep their traditional culture.

The U.S. Supreme Court said the Oneida have the right to sue to get back lands taken from them illegally.

The Oneida have said they do not want to make

43

a single non-Indian move off their land. They do want justice, though. To survive as a nation, they must have land. The agreement will probably involve land owned by the state of New York.

Even before this good news, the Oneida had changed their lives. Today, they have nursing homes, early education programs, better housing, day care, libraries, and schools. Businesses are prospering.

More and more Oneida

Richard Chrisjohn, Sr. (left), is one of two Oneida Nation representatives in the New York legislature. Oneida children look forward to the day when their nation is united again.

are returning to their ancestral lands. The Standing Stone, now on its tiny spot of land in New York, may someday again point the way for a united Oneida people.

WORDS YOU SHOULD KNOW

adopt (uh•DAHPT) — to take in; to make part of the family

ancestor (AN•sess•ter) — a grandparent or forebear earlier in history

attorney (uh•TER•nee) — a person trained in the law; a lawyer

ceremony (SAIR•ih•moh•nee) — a celebration or a religious service

clan (KLAN) — a group of related families descended from a common ancestor or spirit

confederacy (kun•FED•er•uh•see) — a union of nations, states, or people joined together for some purpose

constitution (kahn•stih•TOO•shun) — a set of rules or laws for the government of a group of people

council (KOWN•sil) — a meeting held to discuss problems and to decide a course of action

descendant (dih•SEN•dint) — a child or a grandchild; a person who comes later in a family line

explore (ex•PLOHR) — to travel in an unfamiliar place to find out about the land and the people there

foreigners (FOR•in•erz) — people from other countries

government (GUV•ern•mint) — a plan for ruling a nation, a state, or a town or city; the people who rule

industrial (in•DUSS•tree•il) — manufacturing of goods such as automobiles, furniture, and machinery

issues (ISH•ooz) — problems to be talked about and settled

league (LEEG) — a group of nations or people joined together for some purpose

missionaries (MISH•un•air•eez) — persons sent out by a church to spread their religion

nation (NAY•shun) — a group of people who share a common language, customs, beliefs, and way of life

neutral (NOO•tril) — not favoring one side or the other

organization (or•guh•nih•ZAY•shun) — a group of persons joined together for some purpose

rebel (REH • bil) — a person who fights against a government or other authority

representative (rep • prih • ZEN • ta • tihv) — a person who acts and speaks for a group of people

reservation (rez • er • VAY • shun) — a piece of land reserved or kept by the government as a home for Indians

smallpox (SMALL • pahx) — a disease that is often fatal and that is easily spread from one person to another

territory (TAIR • ih • tor • ee) — an area of land that a group of people regard as their own

totem (TOH • tim) — an animal or a natural object used by a family or other group to represent them; a picture; a symbol

traditional (truh • DISH • un • il) — following old customs and beliefs

INDEX

American Revolution, 22, 23, 24, 25, 26, 27, 28
ancestors, 11
Archiquette, Oscar, 38
attorneys, Oneida, 43
Bennett, Robert R., 38
bingo hall, 42
British, 22, 26-27
Cayuga, 8
ceremonies, 11, 41
chiefs, 16, 21, 22, 28
children, 11, 18
cookhouse, 42

Christians, Oneida as, 25, 26
clans, 11, 15-16, 28
Clinton, Governor, 40
Congress (U.S.), 29, 32
constitution, Oneida, 36
councils, 10, 41
crops, 17-18
disease, 20, 32
Duck Creek, Wisconsin, 32
Europeans, 4, 8, 19
farming, 6-7, 17
fishing, 17

furs, **19**
General Allotment Act, **32**
government, Oneida, **10, 16, 28,
30, 33, 34, 35, 36, 37**
Haudenosaunee, **8, 10, 19, 20,
23, 30**
history of the Oneida, **11, 12, 13**
Indian Reorganization Act, **35-36**
Iroquois Confederacy, **8-10, 21-
22, 23, 24, 26, 27, 39**
Johnson, Lyndon B., **39**
Johnson, Sir William, **26, 27**
Kirkland, Reverend Samuel, **25, 26**
land, buying back, **36**
land, sale of, **29, 30, 33-34**
leaders, **37-39**
longhouses, **6, 10, 13-14, 15, 16,
41**
men, **16, 18**
meetings of the Iroquois
Confederacy, **10, 16**
missionaries, **25**
Mohawk, **9, 10, 31**
Moore, Irene, **38**
New York reservation, **40-42,
43-44**
New York State, **9, 30, 44, 45**

Onayotekaono, **5**
Onondaga, **8, 9, 10**
Parker, Ely S., **38, 39**
peace, **10**
Powless, Purcell, **38**
Roosevelt, Franklin D., **35**
Seneca, **8, 10, 39**
Shenandoah, Peter, **26**
Standing Stone, **5-6, 24, 41, 45**
Superintendent of Indian Affairs,
British, **26-27**
totems, **15-16**
Tuscarora, **9, 10, 26, 29**
U.S. Bureau of Indian Affairs
(BIA), **39**
U.S. government, Oneida and,
29-30, 32-34, 43-44
U.S. Supreme Court, **34, 43**
Van den Bogaert, Harmen
Meyndertsz, **12, 13, 18**
village life, **4, 6, 13-18**
war, **20, 21-24, 32**
Washington, George, **29**
Williams, Eleazer, **31**
Wisconsin, reservation in, **31-32,
33, 34, 35, 36, 37, 39**
women, **15, 16, 17, 28**

About the Author

Jill Duvall is a political scientist who received an M.A. from Georgetown University in 1976. Since then, her research and writing have included a variety of national and international issues. Among these are world hunger, alternative energy, human rights, cross-cultural and interracial relationships. One of her current endeavors is a study of ancient goddess cultures. Ms. Duvall proudly serves as a member of the Board of Managers of the Glenn Mills Schools, a facility that is revolutionizing methods for rehabilitating male juvenile delinquents.